TEAM SPIRIT ®

SMART BOOKS FOR YOUNG FANS

THE BOSTON CELTICS

BY
MARK STEWART

NORWOOD HOUSE PRESS
CHICAGO, ILLINOIS

Norwood House Press
P.O. Box 316598
Chicago, Illinois 60631

For information regarding Norwood House Press, please visit our website at:
www.norwoodhousepress.com or call 866-565-2900.

All photos courtesy of Associated Press except the following:
TCMA, Inc. (6, 42 top), The Sporting News (7, 17), Editions Rencontre (9),
TIME Inc./Sports Illustrated (15, 23), Boston Celtics (21, 33), JBC/NBA Hoops (22),
Capitol Card Co. (24), Topps, Inc. (26, 34 right, 35 left, 42 bottom, 45), The Star Company (35 top),
Dell Publishing (36), Prentice-Hall, Inc. (37), Black Book (38, 41),
NBA Players Association (39), Fleer Corp. (40), Author's Collection (43).
Cover Photo: Michael Dwyer/Associated Press

The memorabilia and artifacts pictured in this book are presented for educational and informational purposes,
and come from the collection of the author.

Editor: Mike Kennedy
Designer: Ron Jaffe
Project Management: Black Book Partners, LLC.
Special thanks to Topps, Inc.

Library of Congress Cataloging-in-Publication Data

Stewart, Mark, 1960 July 7-
  The Boston Celtics / by Mark Stewart.
    pages cm. -- (Team spirit)
  Includes bibliographical references and index.
  Summary: "A revised Team Spirit Basketball edition featuring the Boston
Celtics that chronicles the history and accomplishments of the team.
Includes access to the Team Spirit website which provides additional
information and photos"-- Provided by publisher.
  ISBN 978-1-59953-630-9 (library edition : alk. paper) -- ISBN
978-1-60357-639-0 (ebook)
  1. Boston Celtics (Basketball team)--Juvenile literature. 2.
Basketball--Massachusetts--Boston--Juvenile literature. I. Title.
  GV885.52.B67S74 2014
  796.323'640974461--dc23
                                              2014003844

253N—072014
Manufactured in the United States of America in North Mankato, Minnesota.

COVER PHOTO: Few teams in basketball history can match the Celtics when it comes to team spirit.

Table of Contents

ABOUT OUR GLOSSARY

In this book, there may be several words that you are reading for the first time. Some are sports words, some are new vocabulary words, and some are familiar words that are used in an unusual way. All of these words are defined on page 46. Throughout the book, sports words appear in **bold type**. Regular vocabulary words appear in ***bold italic type***.

Meet the Celtics

If you want to experience a winning *tradition*, go to a Boston Celtics game and tilt your head up. There, hanging from the rafters of the arena, is one championship banner after another. Other banners show the uniform numbers of the team's great stars of the past.

The Celtics are one of the oldest and most successful teams in sports history. They have won championships in five different *decades*—the 1950s, 1960s, 1970s, 1980s, and in the first decade of the 21st century. They have smashed records and broken barriers, and made green and white the unofficial colors of basketball.

This book tells the story of the Celtics. Their dedication to winning through unselfish team play sets an example for every player wearing the Boston uniform. It also serves as a reminder to other teams in the **National Basketball Association (NBA)**—and in all sports—that excellence is a goal well worth shooting for.

Kris Humphries and Jeff Green battle for a rebound in a 2013–14 game. The Celtics take pride in winning as a team.

Glory Days

During the 1920s and 1930s, the sport of **professional** basketball struggled to attract loyal fans. High school and college games were much more popular. However, in the years after World War II, the pro game started to make headlines across the United States. A new league called the **Basketball Association of America (BAA)** formed in 1946. It later merged with the **National Basketball League** to form the NBA. One of the new league's driving forces was Walter Brown. He owned the BAA's club in Boston, which he named the Celtics.

After struggling for a few years, the Celtics became a winning team during the 1950–51 season. Three new faces made the difference—coach Red Auerbach, guard Bob Cousy, and center Ed Macauley. Auerbach came to Boston with the belief that a fast-paced offense could win championships. At the time, there was no **shot clock** in the NBA.

Most teams held the ball for a long time, waiting for an easy scoring chance. With Macauley grabbing rebounds and throwing long passes to Cousy, the Celtics were able to beat opponents down the court for quick baskets.

In 1956, the Celtics traded for a young center named Bill Russell. He was a ferocious defensive player and a great rebounder—perfect for Auerbach's system. With Russell shutting down opponents on defense and Cousy leading the charge on offense, Boston was practically unstoppable. Russell and Cousy made up the heart of a club that included other fine players, such as Bill Sharman, Frank Ramsey, Tom Heinsohn, and Jim Loscutoff. Boston won the NBA championship in 1956–57, lost in the **NBA Finals** in 1957–58, and then went on an amazing streak. From 1958–59 to 1968–69, the Celtics were NBA champions 10 times!

Auerbach was a genius when it came to fitting new players into his system. As *veterans* retired, they were replaced by talented stars that

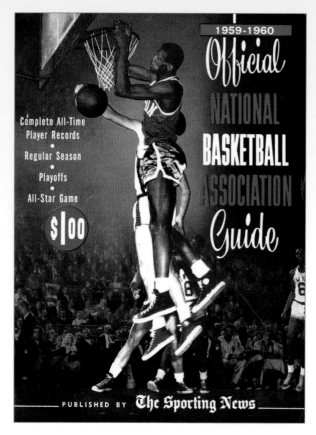

LEFT: Bob Cousy led Boston's fast-paced offense.   **ABOVE**: Bill Russell soars above the rim on the cover this NBA guide.

included Sam Jones, K.C. Jones, Bailey Howell, Don Nelson, Satch Sanders, and John Havlicek. Most years, it seemed as if the Celtics barely broke a sweat on their way to the championship.

During the 1970s, a new *generation* of Celtics took over. Havlicek and Nelson were now the leaders of a group that included center Dave Cowens, guard Jo Jo White, and forward Paul Silas. The Celtics played for the **Eastern Conference** championship six years

Basketball

Dave Cowens

in a row and advanced to the NBA Finals twice (in 1974 and 1976). Boston won the title both years.

The Celtics continued to play championship basketball in the 1980s. The team reached the NBA Finals five times and won three league titles. Boston's star player was a smart and talented forward named Larry Bird. Time and again, he made the winning play for the Celtics. Bird's teammates included Kevin McHale and Robert Parish. They played their best when they were close to the

LEFT: Larry Bird was at his best with the game on the line.
ABOVE: Dave Cowens led Boston to a pair of NBA titles in the 1970s.

basket. Boston's "Big Three" got plenty of help from role players such as Nate "Tiny" Archibald, Cedric Maxwell, Gerald Henderson, Dennis Johnson, Bill Walton, M.L. Carr, and Danny Ainge.

After 40 years of winning, the Celtics began to struggle in the 1990s. Boston tried to rebuild through the NBA **draft**. The team found two great players in the 1990s—Reggie Lewis and Len Bias—but tragedy struck twice. Lewis died suddenly from a heart ailment. Bias died from a drug overdose. These sad losses left the club with a hole it simply could not fill.

Eight years of losing finally came to an end in 2001–02. The Celtics welcomed a new group of talented young players to Boston, led by forwards Paul Pierce and Antoine Walker. Pierce proved to be a special player. He kept pressure on opponents by attacking the basket again and again. But Pierce alone was not enough to get Boston back to the NBA Finals. The team finally decided it needed more star power.

Prior to the 2007–08 season, the Celtics made a series of deals that brought superstars Kevin Garnett and Ray Allen to Boston. Just as in the team's glory years, Pierce, Garnett, and Allen set the example for the young players—including guard Rajon Rondo, who would soon become Boston's leader. Under coach Doc Rivers, the Celtics returned to the NBA Finals in 2008 and beat the Los Angeles Lakers to win their 17th championship.

Two years later, the Celtics played for the title again, but they fell in seven games to Los Angeles. In the years that followed, Pierce, Garnett, and Allen left the Celtics to make room for younger players. The team brought in a new coach to lead the next generation of stars. With a proud past and bright future, Boston fans can hardly wait for the next Celtics *dynasty*.

LEFT: Paul Pierce, Ray Allen, and Kevin Garnett continued the Boston tradition of hardnosed, winning basketball.
ABOVE: Rajon Rondo looks for an opening in the defense.

Home Court

The Celtics played their first 50 seasons in the Boston Garden. In its time, it was one of the best-known sports arenas in America. Celtics fans loved the "Garden" because they could get very close to the action on the court. In 1957, it became the first arena to host the NBA Finals and Stanley Cup Finals (the championship of pro hockey) at the same time.

In 1995, the Celtics moved into a new home. They didn't have to go very far—the "new Garden" was built just inches away from the old one. One thing that didn't change was Boston's famous parquet floor. This style of court uses different shades of wood to form an eye-catching design.

BY THE NUMBERS

- *The Celtics' arena has 18,624 seats for basketball.*
- *At the start of the 2013–14 season, 21 "retired" jerseys hung from the ceiling of the new Boston Garden: 00, 1, 2, 3, 6, 10, 14, 15, 16, 17, 18, 19, 21, 22, 23, 24, 25, 31, 32, 33, and 35—plus LOSCY (for Jim Loscutoff) and MIC (for announcer Johnny Most).*

Banners celebrating Boston's championships and the team's best players can be seen hanging from the ceiling in the new Garden.

Dressed for Success

The Celtics and their fans love their team's many traditions. That includes their uniforms. For more than 60 seasons, the team has worn white with green trim at home, and green with white trim on the road. The home uniform has *Celtics* written across the front. The word *Boston* appears on their road uniforms. Today, Boston also wears uniforms with black highlights.

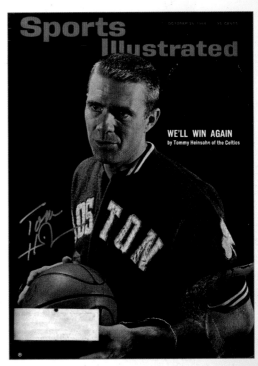

The Boston **logo** is one of the most recognizable in sports. It shows a leprechaun, which is a make-believe character from Irish legends. The first logo was drawn in 1950 by Zang Auerbach, the brother of coach Red Auerbach. To honor Boston's Irish **heritage**, the Celtics have also used a shamrock as a team symbol.

LEFT: Avery Bradley heads down the court in Boston's 2013–14 home uniform.
ABOVE: Tom Heinsohn signed this *Sports Illustrated*, which shows him in the team's green and white colors.

15

We Won!

Before the Celtics won their first championship, Boston basketball fans believed that the team was just one good player away from greatness. Each spring from 1953 to 1955, the Celtics fell just short of a trip to the NBA Finals. In 1956, Boston found the player who put the team over the top. Bill Russell was a slightly awkward center who competed with amazing speed and passion. On any other team, Russell's talent might have been wasted. On the Celtics, he was a perfect fit. Russell blocked shots, hauled down rebounds, and fired long passes that led to easy baskets. Coach Red Auerbach believed that a team built around the fast break could be unbeatable. He was right.

The Celtics faced the St. Louis Hawks in the 1957 NBA Finals in the spring of Russell's first season. The series was not decided until Game 7. The Celtics and Hawks played two thrilling **overtimes** before Boston won, 125–123. The Hawks got revenge by winning the 1958 NBA Finals. After that, the Celtics won the NBA championship eight years in a row. Only once during

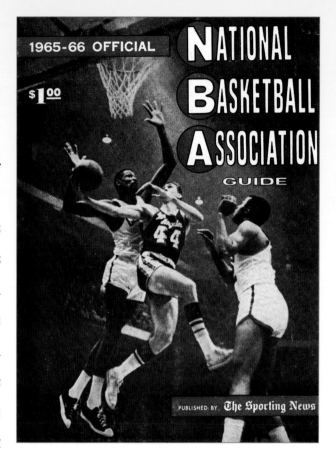

This NBA Guide shows Boston's great defense against the Lakers in the 1965 finals. The Celtics beat Los Angeles in that series.

that span were the Celtics ever seriously challenged.

Five of Boston's NBA titles came against the Los Angeles Lakers. In 1962, the Celtics faced a tough task. Trailing the Lakers after five games, Boston needed to win back-to-back games to take the championship. The Celtics cruised to victory in Game 6, but Game 7 was a different story. The teams battled to the last second of the fourth quarter, and the contest went into overtime. The Celtics pulled together for a 110–107 victory.

Boston added many more championships during Russell's career. For most fans, his last two titles were the sweetest of all. In 1967–68, many of the Celtics looked old and tired. They did not finish in first place in the Eastern Conference. However, once the **playoffs** began, Boston came alive. Russell, by this time a **player-coach**, guided his teammates to victory over the Lakers in the

NBA Finals. The following season, the Celtics took the same path to the championship. After another lackluster regular season, Boston got hot in the **postseason** and beat Los Angeles for the title.

The Celtics captured their next championship in 1974. John Havlicek and Dave Cowens were now the team leaders. They were spectacular in Game 7 of the NBA Finals, sparking Boston to a hard-fought victory over Kareem Abdul-Jabbar and the Milwaukee Bucks.

Two years later, Jo Jo White was the star when Boston won its 13th NBA title, this time against the Phoenix Suns. One of the games in that series went into triple-overtime. For many fans, it is still the most exciting contest ever played in the NBA Finals.

During the 1980s, the Celtics won three more championships, thanks to their "Big Three" of Larry Bird, Kevin McHale, and Robert Parish. They combined with a talented supporting cast to make Boston a tough team to beat. Players such as Cedric Maxwell—who was named **Most Valuable Player (MVP)** of the

1981 NBA Finals—carried on the team's great winning tradition of rising to the occasion when the pressure was greatest.

Boston's championship series against the Lakers in 1984 was one of the most thrilling ever. It featured basketball's best *rivalry*, which pitted Bird against Los Angeles superstar Magic Johnson. Neither team gave an inch. The series went the full seven games, with the Celtics taking the title on their home court. Bird was named the MVP.

Not surprisingly, Celtics fans got very used to winning. But they never imagined they would have to wait 22 years for another championship. Many of the fans who watched Paul Pierce, Kevin Garnett, and Ray Allen beat the Lakers in the 2008 NBA Finals were not even born in the 1980s. Still, they celebrated Boston's 17th NBA championship with all the passion of generations past.

LEFT: Larry Bird and Red Auerbach raise the NBA championship trophy in 1986. **ABOVE**: Paul Pierce can't contain his joy after Boston's 2008 title.

Go-To Guys

To be a true star in the NBA, you need more than a great shot. You have to be a "go-to guy"—someone teammates trust to make the winning play when the seconds are ticking away in a big game. Celtics fans have had a lot to cheer about over the years, including these great stars …

THE PIONEERS

BOB COUSY   6′ 1″ Guard

- BORN: 8/9/1928   • PLAYED FOR TEAM: 1950–51 TO 1962–63

During Bob Cousy's brilliant career, there was not a better ball handler or passer in the NBA. Cousy was a master at running the fast break. He led the Celtics to six championships, was an **All-Star** 13 times, and joined the **Hall of Fame** in 1971.

BILL SHARMAN   6′ 1″ Guard

- BORN: 5/25/1926   • DIED: 10/25/2013   • PLAYED FOR TEAM: 1951–52 TO 1960–61

Bill Sharman believed that practice made perfect. He was one of the NBA's best shooters, and his *stamina* on the court was legendary. Sharman led the NBA in free-throw shooting seven times.

FRANK RAMSEY   6′ 3″ Guard/Forward

• BORN: 7/13/1931   • PLAYED FOR TEAM: 1954–55 & 1956–57 TO 1963–64

Frank Ramsey was Boston's "sixth man"—a player who begins games on the bench and then substitutes for one of his five teammates. He could play just about any position. Ramsey helped Boston win seven NBA titles.

TOM HEINSOHN   6′ 7″ Forward

• BORN: 8/26/1934   • PLAYED FOR TEAM: 1956–57 TO 1964–65

Tom Heinsohn was a smart player with a great shot and a nose for the ball. He was named **Rookie of the Year** in his first season in Boston. Later in the 1970s, he coached the team to two championships.

BILL RUSSELL   6′ 9″ Center

• BORN: 2/12/1934   • PLAYED FOR TEAM: 1956–57 TO 1968–69

Bill Russell was the heart of 11 championship teams in Boston. He was the NBA MVP five times, and also coached the Celtics to league titles in 1968 and 1969. Russell averaged more than 20 rebounds a game during his career.

JOHN HAVLICEK   6′ 5″ Guard/Forward

• BORN: 4/8/1940

• PLAYED FOR TEAM: 1962–63 TO 1977–78

John Havlicek got better and better with age. After more than a decade in the league, he became the NBA's best all-around forward. Havlicek led the Celtics to the NBA title in 1974 and 1976.

RIGHT: John Havlicek

DAVE COWENS   6´ 9˝ Center

- BORN: 10/25/1948   • PLAYED FOR TEAM: 1970–71 TO 1979–80

Dave Cowens looked small compared to other NBA centers of his day. But no one could match his will to win. Cowens was the league MVP in 1972–73. He finished his career with more than 10,000 rebounds.

LARRY BIRD   6´ 9˝ Forward

- BORN: 12/7/1956   • PLAYED FOR TEAM: 1979–80 TO 1991–92

Larry Bird did not look like a superstar, but he played like one. Bird was at his best in close games and loved to take **3-pointers** with the clock winding down. He was voted the Rookie of the Year in 1980 and was named the NBA MVP three seasons in a row.

KEVIN McHALE   6´ 10˝ Forward

- BORN: 12/19/1957
- PLAYED FOR TEAM: 1980–81 TO 1992–93

In 1996, Kevin McHale was named one of the Top 50 players in NBA history. He earned this honor by being almost impossible to defend. When McHale and Robert Parish were on the court together, they gave Boston a huge advantage.

ABOVE: Kevin McHale   **RIGHT**: Rajon Rondo

PAUL PIERCE   6′ 6″ Forward

• BORN: 10/13/1977   • PLAYED FOR TEAM: 1998–99 TO 2012–13

Few players have ever been harder to stop than Paul Pierce. From the moment he joined the Celtics, he proved he could score from anywhere on the court. Pierce was named MVP of the 2008 NBA Finals.

KEVIN GARNETT   6′ 11″ Forward

• BORN: 5/19/1976   • PLAYED FOR TEAM: 2007–08 TO 2012–13

Kevin Garnett entered the NBA in 1995 as a teenager. By the time he joined the Celtics 12 years later, he was one of the league's most respected leaders. Along with Ray Allen, Garnett helped Boston become a championship team.

RAJON RONDO   6′ 1″ Guard

• BORN: 2/22/1986

• FIRST SEASON WITH TEAM: 2006–07

Only a handful of players in Boston history have combined passing, scoring, and defensive skills as well as Rajon Rondo. He set team records for steals and **assists** in 2009–10 and was an All-Star four years in a row. Rondo was the floor leader on Boston's 2008 championship team.

Calling the Shots

The Celtics have one of the most impressive coaching traditions in NBA history. Among those who have led the team are Tom Heinsohn, Bill Fitch, K.C. Jones, Chris Ford, Rick Pitino, and Doc Rivers. All had great insight into the game and inspired their players to perform their best. At one time or another, all of them also worked for the greatest Boston coach of all, Red Auerbach.

Auerbach joined the Celtics for the 1950–51 season. Over the next 16 years, the team never had a losing record. Auerbach created basketball's greatest winning machine. During one 10-year period, Boston took the NBA crown nine times. When Auerbach retired from coaching, he stayed with the Celtics to run the team. In 1966, Auerbach's star center, Bill Russell, became Boston's player-coach. The Celtics won two more championships with Russell in charge.

Auerbach watched proudly from the stands as his team won five more championships in the 1970s and 1980s. Heinsohn was the coach for two of them. He led the Celtics to 68 victories in 1972–73—the most in team history. Fitch coached the Celtics in the early 1980s, molding Larry Bird, Kevin McHale, and Robert Parish into an unstoppable front line. He guided Boston to the NBA title in 1981. Like Heinsohn, Jones was a former Celtic who knew many of Auerbach's championship secrets. Boston played excellent defense with Jones on the sideline, winning two more championships in the 1980s.

Amazingly, Auerbach was also around to see Rivers become Boston's head coach. However, he passed away two years before the Celtics won their next championship, in 2008. Auerbach would have loved the way Rivers led his team. He understood what players go through during a game and also during a season. That helped him make smart decisions and gave the Celtics confidence when the pressure was on. In 2013, Brad Stevens replaced Rivers. Stevens had worked wonders as a college coach. He brought his passion for practice and preparation to the Celtics.

LEFT: Red Auerbach
ABOVE: Doc Rivers celebrates Boston's 2008 championship.

One Great Day

Of all the championships won by the Celtics, their greatest triumph might actually have come in the second round of the 1965 postseason against the Philadelphia 76ers. Earlier in the year, the 76ers had traded for Wilt Chamberlain. No player was more of a challenge to Bill Russell. Chamberlain often scored more points and grabbed more rebounds in their match-ups, but Russell was always focused on winning. Now Chamberlain had a chance to turn the tables on Russell and send the Celtics home early.

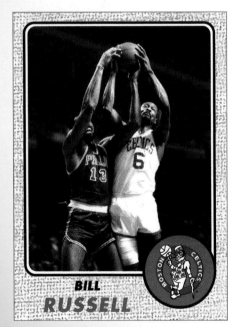

BILL RUSSELL

The series was tied after six games. Game 7 was played in the Boston Garden. The fans cheered as the Celtics opened up an 18-point lead early in the game. The 76ers fought back. Boston led 110–109 with five seconds left to play.

The Celtics had the ball. Russell tried to throw it inbounds from under Boston's basket. But his pass hit a wire holding up the backboard, and the 76ers were awarded the ball. Boston called a timeout to talk strategy. "Man, somebody bail me out!" said an embarrassed Russell.

The Celtics guessed that the 76ers would want to get the ball to Chamberlain. Philadelphia tried to cross up Boston, and instead set up a play for Chet Walker. But no one could fool John Havlicek. As Philadelphia's Hal Greer prepared to pass to Walker, Havlicek leaped high in the air and tipped the ball. Sam Jones of the Celtics grabbed the ball and threw it back to Havlicek. As the final buzzer sounded, Boston announcer Johnny Most screamed again and again, "Havlicek stole the ball!"

The first player to hug Havlicek was Russell. All the big center could say was "Thank you."

LEFT: This trading card shows one of the many battles between Wilt Chamberlain and Bill Russell.   **ABOVE**: Boston fans mob John Havlicek after his famous steal.

Legend Has It

Which Celtic got his nickname from a gun?

LEGEND HAS IT that Tom Heinsohn did. Heinsohn's job on the Celtics was to shoot as often as possible. He reminded fans of the American anti-aircraft guns used in World War II to shoot at enemy planes. The sound those guns made was *ack-ack-ack-ack-ack*. Heinsohn's nickname was—you guessed it—Ack-Ack!

ABOVE: Tom Heinsohn displays the form that helped him earn the nickname "Ack-Ack."

which Celtic refused to let his number be retired?

LEGEND HAS IT that Jim Loscutoff did. Loscutoff was the player who entered games when Bill Russell needed a break. Like Russell, he was an excellent defender. When the Celtics offered to retire Loscutoff's #18, he asked instead that they hang a banner with his nickname—"Loscy"—so that other players could wear his number. Later, the Celtics retired 18 in honor of Dave Cowens, who wore the number during the 1970s.

Which Celtic was "robbed" of an MVP award?

LEGEND HAS IT that Ray Allen was—and the fans were to blame! Allen was the last player added to the 2008 NBA All-Star Game, after teammate Kevin Garnett could not play for the East squad because of an injury. With the West leading late in the game, Allen nailed a 3-pointer to put his team ahead. He made two more long shots to increase the lead, and then scored five more points. The East won, 134–128. Allen led all scorers with 28 points. So who was named the game's MVP? The NBA let the fans text their votes and they picked LeBron James!

It Really Happened

The Celtics never give up, and neither do their fans. Over the years, this attitude has led to many dramatic wins, often with amazing plays in the final seconds. The Celtics produced such a victory over the Detroit Pistons in the 1987 playoffs.

Boston was hosting Detroit in Game 5 of the **Eastern Conference Finals**. The Pistons were a young team with the talent to win the NBA title. The only thing they lacked was championship experience. The Celtics used this to their advantage. Detroit led 107–106 with five seconds left. The team's best player, sure-handed guard Isiah Thomas, had the ball out of bounds under the Boston basket. All he had to do was pass to a teammate, and the Pistons could let the clock tick away.

Larry Bird refused to surrender. When he saw Thomas look at Bill Laimbeer, he sprinted in the big center's direction. Bird got there just in time to tip the ball away. But as he grabbed for it at the sideline, he could not gain his balance. Falling out of bounds, Bird saw a flash of white and green. It was Dennis Johnson. Bird fired the ball into the hands of his teammate.

Dennis Johnson and Larry Bird celebrate a Boston victory.
Their quick thinking produced the dramatic win over the Pistons.

"DJ" corralled the loose ball and made an easy layup with the
clock reading 0:01. The Celtics won the game in miracle fashion,
108–107. The Pistons learned a hard lesson that day. Never count
out the Celtics until the buzzer sounds!

Team Spirit

Fans of the Celtics are as loyal and passionate as they come. They want to win as badly as the players they root for. In the old Boston Garden, the arena used to shake when the fans rose to their feet and cheered their loudest. The same is true today. Boston fans love the Celtics, and they are not shy about showing it.

The Celtics have one of the NBA's most recognizable mascots, Lucky the Leprechaun. In the old days, Lucky would roam the court to get the fans excited. Today, Lucky is also a slam-dunking acrobatic. In 2006, the Celtics Dancers took the floor for the first time. Boston had never had a dance team before. Now it is one of the most popular in the NBA.

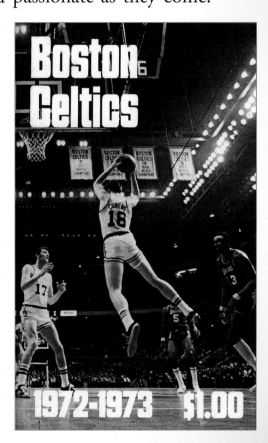

LEFT: Paul Pierce waves to the fans after Boston's 2008 championship.
ABOVE: This Celtics yearbook provides a glimpse of the old Boston Garden.

Timeline

The basketball season is played from October through June. That means each season takes place at the end of one year and the beginning of the next. In this timeline, the accomplishments of the Celtics are shown by season.

1956–57
The Celtics win their first championship.

1965–66
The Celtics win their 8th championship in a row.

1946–47
The Celtics play their first season.

1959–60
Bob Cousy leads the NBA in assists for the eighth year in a row.

1972–73
Dave Cowens is named NBA MVP.

Frank Ramsey was a key player for the 1957 champs.

Don Nelson starred for Boston in the 1960s and 1970s.

Larry
Bird

1985–86
Larry Bird is named
NBA MVP for the
third year in a row.

1995–96
Dino Radja leads the
team in scoring and
rebounds.

2012–13
Rajon Rondo leads the
NBA in assists per game.

1980–81
The Celtics win their
14th championship.

2001–02
Antoine Walker leads the
NBA in minutes played.

2007–08
The Celtics win their
17th championship.

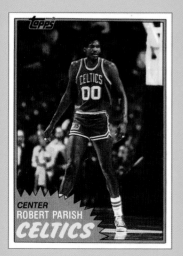

Robert Parish
was a star for
the championship
teams of the 1980s.

Kevin Garnett
celebrates during
the 2007–08 season.

Fun Facts

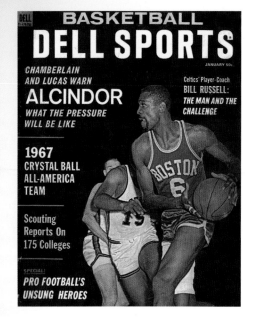

DOUBLE DUTY

In 1966, the Celtics named Bill Russell the team's player-coach. Russell was the first African American head coach of a major American sports team.

THREE'S COMPANY

In a 2010 playoff game against the Cleveland Cavaliers, Rajon Rondo finished with 29 points, 18 rebounds, and 13 assists for a triple-double. The only other players to have double-figures in points, rebounds, and assists in a playoff game were Hall of Famers Oscar Robertson and Wilt Chamberlain.

CRAZY EIGHT

In Game 2 of the 2010 NBA Finals, Ray Allen broke Michael Jordan's record of six 3-pointers in a half. He went on to set a mark for an NBA Finals game with eight 3-pointers.

THE WRITE STUFF

Bill Sharman was an expert on the art of shooting. After his playing days with the Celtics, he wrote a 222-page book on the subject!

FROM THE HEART

In 2011, the Celtics traded for forward Jeff Green. They thought he was the perfect player to fill Paul Pierce's shoes. Doctors later found that Green had a serious heart problem and made him sit out an entire season. Happily, Green returned to the lineup in 2012–13 and had a great year.

HAIL TO THE CHIEF

During the 1980s, Robert Parish led the Celtics in rebounds eight years and was an All-Star seven times. When he retired from the NBA, "The Chief" had played 21 seasons—more than anyone in history.

LEFT: This magazine shows Bill Russell as a player-coach.
ABOVE: Bill Sharman really did "write the book" on shooting.

Talking Basketball

"Winning the championship is the all-time best memory that I will ever have."

▶ **Nate "Tiny" Archibald,** *on Boston's 1981 NBA title*

"Leadership is diving for a loose ball, getting the crowd involved, getting other players involved."

▶ **Larry Bird,** *on leading by example*

"I had guys when I was coaching who were in their thirties, like Cousy, Havlicek, Russell. They were very bright."

▶ **Red Auerbach,** *on why he listened to his veteran players*

"Never **underestimate** the heart of a champion."

▶ **Doc Rivers,** *on the Celtics' winning tradition*

"I appreciated the fans as a player, and I recognized how important they were to us."
► **Jo Jo White,** *on the lift that the Celtics get from their fans*

"The game isn't over 'til the clock says zero."
► **Paul Pierce,** *on playing hard until the final buzzer*

"The MVP award was very satisfying in terms of personal accomplishments, but the championship was the most important thing of all."
► **Bob Cousy,** *on putting the team's success first*

"Star players have an enormous responsibility beyond their statistics—the responsibility to pick up their team and carry it. You have to do this to win championships."
► **Bill Russell,** *on what it means to be a star*

LEFT: Nate Archibald
ABOVE: Jo Jo White

Great Debates

People who root for the Celtics love to compare their favorite moments, teams, and players. Some debates have been going on for years! How would you settle these classic basketball arguments?

Boston's greatest comeback came in the 2002 playoffs ...

Paul Pierce • F

... because they beat the New Jersey Nets after trailing by 21 points in the fourth quarter. New Jersey (now Brooklyn) led 75–53 after three periods. But Antoine Walker and Paul Pierce (**LEFT**) caught fire, and the Nets had no answer. Boston made 11 of 19 shots and hit 18 of 21 free throws. The Celtics launched one of the most startling comebacks in NBA history and won, 94–90.

That was nothing compared to the comeback against the Los Angeles Lakers in Game 4 of the 2008 NBA Finals ...

... because it came against Boston's biggest rival. The Celtics were behind 45–21 in the second quarter—and trailed by 20 in the third period—against a great team playing on its own home court. But the Celtics kept chipping away. James Posey and Eddie House led the charge, as Boston won, 97–91. Five days later, the Celtics took the NBA title.

John Havlicek was the best sixth man in NBA history ...

... because the Celtics won the NBA championship the first four years he played this role. Havlicek (RIGHT) began most games on the bench. When Red Auerbach spotted a weakness in Boston's opponent, he would send in Havlicek to take advantage of the opportunity. He was always on the floor for the Celtics when the final buzzer sounded.

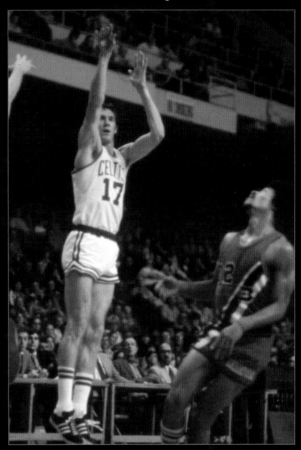

Who do you think Havlicek learned from? Frank Ramsey was the best sixth man ...

... because he filled this role for the Celtics before Havlicek did. Bob Cousy and Bill Sharman would wear opponents down with their fast-paced style, and then Ramsey would come into the game and Boston's lead would increase. Ramsey was a good scorer and rebounder. He often played alongside Cousy and Sharman as a forward. Like Havlicek, he was usually on the floor in the final minutes.

For the Record

The great Celtics teams and players have left their marks on the record books. These are the "best of the best" ...

Bill Sharman

Cedric Maxwell

CELTICS AWARD WINNERS

ROOKIE OF THE YEAR

Tom Heinsohn	1956–57
Dave Cowens	1970–71*
Larry Bird	1979–80

NBA FINALS MVP

John Havlicek	1973–74
Jo Jo White	1975–76
Cedric Maxwell	1980–81
Larry Bird	1983–84
Larry Bird	1985–86
Paul Pierce	2007–08

COACH OF THE YEAR

Red Auerbach	1964–65
Tom Heinsohn	1972–73
Bill Fitch	1979–80

SIXTH MAN AWARD

Kevin McHale	1983–84
Kevin McHale	1984–85
Bill Walton	1985–86

NBA MVP

Bob Cousy	1956–57
Bill Russell	1957–58
Bill Russell	1960–61
Bill Russell	1961–62
Bill Russell	1962–63
Bill Russell	1964–65
Dave Cowens	1972–73
Larry Bird	1983–84
Larry Bird	1984–85
Larry Bird	1985–86

ALL-STAR GAME MVP

Ed Macauley	1950–51
Bob Cousy	1953–54
Bill Sharman	1954–55
Bob Cousy	1956–57
Bill Russell	1962–63
Dave Cowens	1972–73
Nate Archibald	1980–81
Larry Bird	1981–82

DEFENSIVE PLAYER OF THE YEAR

Kevin Garnett	2007–08

* Shared this award with another player.

CELTICS ACHIEVEMENTS

Eastern Division Champions	1956–57	Eastern Division Champions	1967–68
NBA Champions	1956–57	NBA Champions	1967–68
Eastern Division Champions	1957–58	Eastern Division Champions	1968–69
Eastern Division Champions	1958–59	NBA Champions	1968–69
NBA Champions	1958–59	Eastern Conference Champions	1973–74
Eastern Division Champions	1959–60	NBA Champions	1973–74
NBA Champions	1959–60	Eastern Conference Champions	1975–76
Eastern Division Champions	1960–61	NBA Champions	1975–76
NBA Champions	1960–61	Eastern Conference Champions	1980–81
Eastern Division Champions	1961–62	NBA Champions	1980–81
NBA Champions	1961–62	Eastern Conference Champions	1983–84
Eastern Division Champions	1962–63	NBA Champions	1983–84
NBA Champions	1962–63	Eastern Conference Champions	1984–85
Eastern Division Champions	1963–64	Eastern Conference Champions	1985–86
NBA Champions	1963–64	NBA Champions	1985–86
Eastern Division Champions	1964–65	Eastern Conference Champions	1986–87
NBA Champions	1964–65	Eastern Conference Champions	2007–08
Eastern Division Champions	1965–66	NBA Champions	2007–08
NBA Champions	1965–66	Eastern Conference Champions	2009–10

Boston fans bought this souvenir pennant during the 1950s.

Pinpoints

The history of a basketball team is made up of many smaller stories. These stories take place all over the map—not just in the city a team calls "home." Match the pushpins on these maps to the **TEAM FACTS**, and you will begin to see the story of the Celtics unfold!

TEAM FACTS

1 Boston, Massachusetts—*The Celtics have played here since the 1946–47 season.*

2 Union City, New Jersey—*Tom Heinsohn was born here.*

3 Hibbing, Minnesota—*Kevin McHale was born here.*

4 West Baden Springs, Indiana—*Larry Bird was born here.*

5 Cheverly, Maryland—*Jeff Green was born here.*

6 St. Louis, Missouri—*Ed Macauley was born here.*

7 Louisville, Kentucky—*Rajon Rondo was born here.*

8 Monroe, Louisiana—*Bill Russell was born here.*

9 Abilene, Texas—*Bill Sharman was born here.*

10 Eugene, Oregon—*Danny Ainge was born here.*

11 Merced, California—*Ray Allen was born here.*

12 Split, Croatia—*Dino Radja was born here.*

Larry Bird

Glossary

Basketball Words
Vocabulary Words

3-POINTERS—Shots taken from behind the 3-point line.

ALL-STAR—A player selected to play in the annual All-Star Game.

ASSISTS—Passes that lead to baskets.

BASKETBALL ASSOCIATION OF AMERICA (BAA)—The league that started in 1946–47 and later became the NBA.

DECADES—Periods of 10 years; also specific periods, such as the 1950s.

DRAFT—The annual meeting during which NBA teams choose from a group of the best college and foreign players.

DYNASTY—A family, group, or team that maintains power over time.

EASTERN CONFERENCE—A group of teams that play in the East. The winner of the Eastern Conference meets the winner of the Western Conference in the league finals.

EASTERN CONFERENCE FINALS—The playoff series that determines which team from the East will play the best team from the West for the NBA championship.

GENERATION—A period of years roughly equal to the time it takes for a person to be born, grow up, and have children.

HALL OF FAME—The museum in Springfield, Massachusetts where basketball's greatest players are honored. A player voted into the Hall of Fame is sometimes called a "Hall of Famer."

HERITAGE—Something important that is passed down through time.

LOGO—A symbol or design that represents a company or team.

MOST VALUABLE PLAYER (MVP)—The annual award given to the league's best player; also given to the best player in the league finals and All-Star Game.

NATIONAL BASKETBALL ASSOCIATION (NBA)—The professional league that has been operating since 1946–47.

NATIONAL BASKETBALL LEAGUE—An early professional league that played 12 seasons, from 1937–38 to 1948–49.

NBA FINALS—The playoff series that decides the champion of the league.

OVERTIMES—Extra periods played when a game is tied after 48 minutes.

PLAYER-COACH—A person who plays for a team and coaches it at the same time.

PLAYOFFS—The games played after the season to determine the league champion.

POSTSEASON—Another term for playoffs.

PROFESSIONAL—A player or team that plays a sport for money.

RIVALRY—Extremely emotional competition.

ROOKIE OF THE YEAR— The annual award given to the league's best first-year player.

SHOT CLOCK—The clock that keeps track of the amount of time that each team is allowed to have the ball before it must take a shot.

STAMINA—The ability to sustain a long physical effort.

TRADITION—A belief or custom that is handed down from generation to generation.

UNDERESTIMATE—Place too low a value on.

VETERANS—Players with great experience.

FAST BREAK

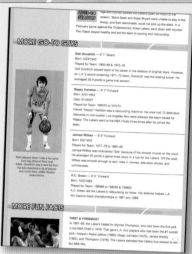

TEAM SPIRIT introduces a great way to stay up to date with your team! Visit our **FAST BREAK** link and get connected to the latest and greatest updates. **FAST BREAK** serves as a young reader's ticket to an exclusive web page—with more stories, fun facts, team records, and photos of the Celtics. Content is updated during and after each season. The **FAST BREAK** feature also enables readers to send comments and letters to the author! Log onto:

www.norwoodhousepress.com/library.aspx

and click on the tab: **TEAM SPIRIT** to access **FAST BREAK**.

Read all the books in the series to learn more about professional sports. For a complete listing of the baseball, basketball, football, and hockey teams in the **TEAM SPIRIT** series, visit our website at:

www.norwoodhousepress.com/library.aspx

On the Road

BOSTON CELTICS
100 Legends Way
Boston, Massachusetts 02114
866-423-5849
www.nba.com/celtics

NAISMITH MEMORIAL BASKETBALL HALL OF FAME
1000 West Columbus Avenue
Springfield, Massachusetts 01105
(877) 4HOOPLA
www.hoophall.com

On the Bookshelf

To learn more about the sport of basketball, look for these books at your library or bookstore:

- Doeden, Matt. *Basketball Legends In the Making*. North Mankato, Minnesota: Capstone Press, 2014.

- Rappaport, Ken. *Basketball's Top 10 Slam Dunkers*. Berkeley Heights, New Jersey: Enslow Publishers, 2013.

- Silverman, Drew. *The NBA Finals*. Minneapolis, Minnesota: ABDO Group, 2013.

Index

PAGE NUMBERS IN **BOLD** REFER TO ILLUSTRATIONS.

THE TEAM

MARK STEWART has written more than 40 books on basketball, and over 150 sports books for kids. He grew up in New York City during the 1960s rooting for the Knicks and Nets, and was lucky enough to meet many of the stars of those teams. Mark comes from a family of writers. His grandfather was Sunday Editor of *The New York Times* and his mother was Articles Editor of *The Ladies' Home Journal* and *McCall's*. Mark has profiled hundreds of athletes over the last 20 years. He has also written several books about his native New York, and New Jersey, his home today. Mark is a graduate of Duke University, with a degree in History. He lives with his daughters and wife Sarah overlooking Sandy Hook, New Jersey.